The Gift of Retirement

THE GIFT

OF RETIREMENT

BY LILIANE GIUDICE

translated by David E. Green

JOHN KNOX PRESS
Richmond, Virginia

This book is a translation of *Der Tag der Pensionierung,* published by Kreuz-Verlag, Stuttgart, Germany, 1971.

Library of Congress Cataloging in Publication Data

Giudice, Liliane, 1913-
   The gift of retirement.

   Translation of Der Tag der Pensionierung.
   1. Aged—Prayer-books and devotions—English.
I. Title.
BV4580.G5813   242   73-5344
ISBN 0-8042-2070-0

CONTENTS

To roam about, to discover in a dream a region crying out to be explored, to have time for those you love, to enjoy the precious leisure of being idle while others work—everything you have spent your lifetime unable to do is dropped in your lap like a disconcerting present upon retirement. You hardly dare to be so happy. The notion that a man is tossed on the scrap heap when he retires, that he must endure his freedom as a kind of drudgery, that his wife finds spending the day with him a burden to be shouldered the rest of her life, that both of them tremble with dread at the thought of the empty hours ahead—this can only be a bad dream or a hallucination.

Here on this earth the hour can never strike when there is nothing left to do; the moment can never arrive when there is no more joy to be found in nature, in art, in study; the hour can never strike that marks the end. It only marks the beginning of a new day.

Nowadays happy people are suspected of being a bit simple-minded. I would nevertheless like to describe a single happy day, a day when nothing special happens, our first day of retirement. It seems to me that it takes more strength to be happy than to put up with being unhappy, for unhappiness flourishes in the soil of passivity, while happiness requires activity.

When you go for a walk in the fall, you may break off a branch here and there, smooth or covered with thorns, stoop to examine another with red or yellow foliage, attracted by its tints or bizarre shape, and, on returning home, arrange them all in a vase. In like manner I have chosen a few of my many unspoken conversations with my husband and found a place for them in our first happy day of retirement.

MORNING

The Giant Caterpillar

It's five past six; the alarm clock hasn't rung. Now our days will no longer begin with its clatter. But you are awake out of long habit. You have turned over and said quietly: "Today they all have to get up, forty-one thousand workers and employees—today they all have to go to work and I can stay in bed."

You have waited forty-three years for this moment. Are you stretching now and enjoying your first moments of ease, just as you had pictured it? Why don't we give a party? Mr. and Mrs. G. request the pleasure of your company on the day of retirement. The bread in the sandwiches you will nibble, the wine in the glasses you will sip—today they are no longer earned by the sweat of the head of our household but by the sweat of forty-one thousand workers and employees. We are sorry for them, but someday they too will be able to celebrate this day.

And why not? It would not be a ceremony honoring you for the work you've done, like the ceremony yesterday at the factory club, but a celebration in our home because from now on you won't have to work. How would you like that?

You're so quiet. I wonder whether you're disappointed or preoccupied. For my part, I'm a bit excited. The day so long awaited—how shall we begin it? Maybe we should even celebrate a little at breakfast? I could light the candles in our candlesticks. We really ought to do something special, don't you think?

I think it will turn into a confusing day. What could you be thinking about now? Of course, I won't really ask you to tell me. Today, just like any other day, I would rather not invade your thoughts. I will only observe you from without, surreptitiously and warily. That's all right, isn't it? And wait to see what you will say to me. I am curious about our first conversation. But I'm surprised you're so quiet!

Oh! You've fallen asleep again! Just fallen asleep and turned off your thoughts. Taking it easy! But I am a bit upset—to fall asleep at this historic moment! I almost think it seems quite natural to you. Once again, your reaction isn't what I'd expected. If I'd asked you out loud, you would have smiled like a rogue, waved the question away, and pulled the blankets over your head.

Now I'm lying here beside you, like the wife of the Chinese poet Po Chü-i, "still far from getting up," who charmed me so yesterday: ". . . and my precious wife, it seems to me, considers me a giant caterpillar, waiting as a pupa for its spring."

My giant caterpillar—now you really have become a pupa. I can't see you anymore. I know from my biology lessons that you are undergoing a mysterious transformation: a creature still imperfect is preparing for its better stage. Will I know you when you leave your cocoon? It spelled constraint for you, but also protection. How will you feel when you may fly instead of crawling? Have you thought too lightly of being free?

It makes me uneasy to think of your mysterious, invisible, silent transformation. You let me lie here beside you full of suspense, and all I can do is wait for my giant caterpillar to burst from his cocoon.

Now They Go to Work

The water is boiling. You will soon dash in, grab the handles of the tray with our breakfast on it, and juggle it into your room. Perhaps, if you catch my distrustful glance, you will laugh and balance the tray a little more precariously, imitating a sailor on a rough sea, finally, with at most a few drops of coffee splashed about, setting it down quite carefully, looking as gentle as a lamb. Perhaps today something totally different will occur to you—to sweep away a little spilled liquid, a few crumbs dropped on the floor, the whole tyranny of everything inconsequential while the morning is still young.

The sound of your footsteps in the bedroom has stopped, but you don't come bursting in. Are you, too, standing at the window like me?

Now they're going to work. The women and children are opening the garage doors, the motors are starting. Some are already waiting at the bus stop, where we no longer have to join them. There he comes now with a smile on his face, still wearing the same suit—the professor with five daughters to educate, who has a pleasantry to celebrate in his southern accent with everyone he passes at this early hour. The chronometer man pops open the cover of his watch, checks the time with everyone waiting in line. Once again today his enigmatic concentration keeps him from noticing how the others politely hide their ironic smiles. Even the former bachelor, who always kept us up-to-date on politics, has to tell what time he has—but first he reaches for his hat, which he can raise so elegantly. Is that the reason he always wears it? He always had such stylish girl friends, until he surprised us with a homely wife, a casserole queen, as you call her.

The secretary, who was my daily fashion column, condescends to approach with dainty steps; she dispenses only a silent nod. She almost missed her bus again, the pretty factory girl with her curly black hair. She's finally risen to employee status by attending evening classes, and is now wavering between one boyfriend who's a mechanic and another who's a doctor. Fragments of destinies on their way to work, fragments whose outcome we will never witness now. Next door, across the street, all around, they are leaving. I wonder what your thoughts are.

You didn't like your occupation; you would rather have become a doctor or a singer. Your Italian teacher would have trained you and waited to be repaid until you were finally standing on a famous stage. But the First World War put an end to your dreams, robbed your father of his position, banished your parents from Egypt with their four daughters, and you had to choose the occupation that promised a good salary soonest.

You must be standing at the window; it's so quiet in the next room. Are you reflecting now on having spent forty-five years selling dyes while wanting to relieve men of their pain or cheer them with song? You have always been at people's disposal, as a student, as a soldier, as a salesman. Forty-five years of earning a living at a job you didn't like. Are you feeling bitter now? I know you have been gnawed by bitterness at times.

Bitterness is something you cannot escape by your own efforts, and no one can remove it from you. There is only one who can deliver from it. Is He approaching you now? In His sight it does not matter whether you liked the job at which you earned your living; even success is unimportant, for He justifies your life just as it is, so that your pleasure or displeasure in your work pales into insignificance, like a children's game.

The Silent Dialogue

Thank heavens I didn't set out the candles! I should have realized that you don't have to camouflage yourself in a proper suit every morning anymore, and that for our first breakfast in peace you would put on your old leather jacket and your worn-out flannel trousers that never stay pressed for more than a day. And you're wearing the wooden sandals that you like so much to clatter about the house in.

Perhaps they remind you of the years in Japan, where you often had to take off your shoes to enter a house, or of your childhood in Alexandria, where your harshest punishment was not being able to run around barefoot during vacation. It reminds me of my old Spanish schoolmate, who with his gray beard and wearing a dinner jacket not long ago greeted his guests barefoot. Whether he had to go barefoot or only did it to shock people, one thing is sure: the directors of his firm didn't like it, and now he regrets what he did. Even a manager can't take too many liberties.

But now it would be all right for you to receive your guests barefoot. You cannot be dismissed from your position of retirement, even if everyone thinks your actions qualify you for commitment. Now you could venture anything, almost anything, you've been forbidden to do throughout your life. Strange that I've never heard of anyone doing something quite mad upon retirement, something he would enjoy tremendously. Are a man's longings deadened as the years go by, or is their shabbiness unmasked?

You sit there in front of me, easy but alert, a combination so natural to you. What will you set about now? If you were a caveman, from Altamira say, perhaps the man who painted that wild horse with the slender head whose grace still enchants us millennia later—in other words, a sensitive man, not uncouth, the kind of man I would have liked even then—you would presumably leave our cave after breakfast, you would go fishing or hunting for our sustenance, and none would say you nay as long as you could bend your bow or hold your club, for life and work would be all one. But today the bow is taken from your hand, others go hunting for us, for our nourishment—and what will you set about doing?

I will not put that question to you. Has your life also known so many dialogues that never are expressed in words? I've often wished for a Cyrano to choose the best of my thoughts and lend them expression at the proper moment. I must feel it myself, when I should speak and what words I should say. When I was a girl it was shyness that restrained my speech; now it is caution. Not as though I were afraid that you might misunderstand me: even when we surprise each other with things we did not expect, it is never an action or a word, anything at all, to separate us, because the one cannot enter into the other's feelings. As from an inexhaustible well, joy streams from you to me, and I think that I, too, enrich your life a bit. There is a giving and receiving in eager communication, but also in silent conversation. There are things that thrive only in silent dialogue, and none must rob another of the experience of letting a thought mature in silent solitude.

The Empty Desk

You've carried out our old brass wastebasket full of surplus letters and documents, and when I go by your door I hear you still at work tearing up paper. You're giving your desk a thorough housecleaning. Soon there'll be nothing on top of it. You never did want any pictures or flowers. Only the Chinese vase with the blue lettering, whose meaning we shall never learn, will continue to do duty as a desk lamp. You may also still have use for the large pewter tray with its monogram of people long dead, where you like to toss unpleasant and unfinished business.

A polished desk top exercises a peculiar fascination. On it one equips oneself with knowledge to deal with life, writes letters of love and of sadness, accounts for one's money, and composes one's last will. On this rectangular surface a portion of our life is determined. When my desk burned in the war, and the flames through the window licked at its ancient Renaissance frieze and at the yellow roses that whirled about in confusion with the papers, I bade farewell to an intimate friend.

Now your desk will soon be neat and empty. Writing to friends, checking a bank statement, filling out a tax return once a year—these cannot fill it. I could set out the old ashtray or your briefcase to hide the emptiness, but you would not like it.

Empty—emptiness is a source of strength. Empty means being free for something. Like the absorbing emptiness of Japanese watercolors or the asceticism of a line drawing by Cézanne. Emptiness must be a challenge, gratifying or devastating.

Up to now you've worked at that desk in the factory, which you left yesterday in another's charge, fighting with some and against others to sell dyes. Carloads of dyes, dyes that are always new, always improved, had to be marketed throughout the world, and filled your days with work and worry. When your friend was discharged, his wife asked the company for his desk. No one had ever expressed such a wish, but how right she was with her loving instinct: the desk stands isolated and almost ugly in the midst of the works of art that fill their home, but your friend is happy at it!

Now you're sitting at your own desk without anything to face. You are alone in the empty space about you, and totally free with the strength life's struggle has left you. In this freedom you will learn something terrible: your dependence, your utter dependence, on sickness and death. Both have lain in wait for you since birth, but not so undisguised, so close, so terrifyingly close. They were always embellished by the ceaseless need to be busy; you were always distracted by work and people. Physicians can control a few diseases, can delay death a little. But what difference does it make? They will never abolish the great end that comes to everything earthly. You are completely dependent on death. Retirement is a disquieting quiet, awaiting the quiet of death.

And now He makes his appearance once more, quite naturally—or else nothingness. If He does not exist, your death is the end of you. Now you must face Him or nothingness. Now you must *believe*, even if you rebel, must believe in transitoriness or in eternity, for you will never *know* until death.

You are sitting at your desk without anything to face. You no longer have to fight with or against others; you must only wrestle with yourself. Here you can no longer blame circumstances, your job, other people; you alone will decide which you will fight to gain, with vigor and with passion. Is that not the only fight that matters? Your struggle is for the crucial stance of your life, almost forgotten amid the competition of business: your stance when you confront Him.

The Word

We have no name for Him, only a word.

We cannot name someone after Him. There are languages in which parents may have the boldness to set their child in relationship to Him at baptism, as a prayer, as a mandate: Gotthelf, Theodore. They are not afraid lest constant repetition distress the child or deaden his responsiveness.

Theologians can pronounce the word without inhibition; they must formulate it over and over again, for it is the subject of their discipline. They work with it as mathematicians work with an unknown, and have juggled it for well-nigh two thousand years. Even those who insist the word does not exist still juggle it; they are like a juggler standing on a stage moving his arms dexterously, as though he had a ball, all the while assuring the audience that he has none.

But we who are not scholars and not jugglers, how are we to act? Shall we let the word pass our lips with ease, as though the ineffable were obvious, or shall we tremble because when spoken aloud it bursts through our everyday existence? No one can evade deciding whether he will whisper the word or proclaim it aloud or shout it down or hush it up, for no one can ignore the word.

Then . . .

"Has the paper come?" you asked me when I placed the flowers on your dresser. A banal question—but what happens when the paper has come? Then the mail comes, then lunch comes, then the evening news comes. The day is stretched over "thens" as on a frame.

We cultivate this "then" even with the children. "When Christmas is here," we say, until they almost burst with anticipation, "then you will see your presents." Later it is "When you go to school," or "When you get a job," or "When you are promoted"—always this anticipation, as at Christmas, that things will be better when one knows more, has more money, holds a higher position. But if we consider soberly and logically, we shall one day stand at the turning point where we must say, starting on some certain day, perhaps the day of retirement: From now on no more promotions, less money, less strength, and then comes death. And now this "then" can turn into an incubus.

For this "then" means that we are unfulfilled in the present moment, and we are buoyed up with the hope of something wonderful, not knowing whether we shall ever live to see this "then." We allow ourselves to be scourged like slaves by "when" and "then" as though freedom will be granted us in the end—or is it only anguish?

Are we so prone to take refuge in "then" because we have a guilty conscience and sense that we cannot adequately fulfill the present moment? And yet the present moment is *all* we have. Now, at least, in retirement, we should have the courage to free ourselves from "then" and find strength to live in the present, to fill the moment with leisure or activity in natural succession.

How the saying seeks to intrude here that I always pushed aside because I cannot fulfill it: The Kingdom of God is within you! It could be in you and in me, *now*, not *then* . . .

Magic

When you brought the money I had asked you for to give the mailman and it was suddenly gone, vanished from your hand before my very eyes, I was so startled that I didn't realize what had happened until I saw you smiling slyly: you had done a magic trick! Then I was so delighted that you had to repeat it for me, even though I already knew what was coming and that the coin was simply hidden somewhere in your fingers or up your sleeve. What was there about this magic that held me so enthralled? Dexterity, illusion, the chance to see something that cannot be?

Ever since that evening when one of our guests suddenly and unexpectedly began to perform magic tricks while we were drinking our after-dinner coffee and delighted us all with his sleight of hand, I have thought that your hands must be made for magic. Our guest was a master among amateur magicians, and held high rank in the magicians' brotherhood. I was pleased to learn that this busy and wealthy industrialist spent every moment practicing—at home, on a plane, sitting at his desk at work, or wherever—even if only doing finger exercises to keep his hands supple. Putting in hard work in order to give his magic the appearance of a game, a game that perishes even as it happens. Music, theater, much that has been shaped by dint of laborious effort perishes in the very moment it gives us joy.

I love Matisse's picture *Le Jeu*. The picture contains nothing to please my taste; the ugly dark piano, the busy wallpaper, the garish carpet, the people's clothes—I find none of them attractive. But for this very reason perhaps it does a wonderful job of capturing for me the theme to which all these are only accompaniment; the woman at the piano, presumably tinkling out a cheap melody, the boys lost in their game of checkers—they are all playing, absorbed, enraptured. What they are playing does not matter, but it brings peace and joy.

To do something to no purpose, to perform magic not because one is bored and seeks distraction, no, simply because it is refreshing! A coin vanishes into thin air, a woman is sawed in half and comes out smiling—everything forbidden by the laws of nature takes place. The magician is like a cunning demigod who can abolish the laws of nature with a snap of his fingers. I wait with bated breath; perhaps he will now make the earth disappear or turn it on its nonexistent head, for we are under his spell and can never know where the magic will cease.

Now you, too, are under its spell! When I bought you that book on magic, you put it aside, and today, when I had quite forgotten it, you took me by surprise. Some will say that you're a fool, for you will never achieve the rank of master in a magicians' brotherhood. A fool is wise. In his actions, inexplicable to reason, he is strangely secure.

An African Village

Our neighbor was finally able to send me the postcard she promised from the Azores. Now she is there, where she absolutely had to go. I wonder if she is content when, lifting her head, she eyes the region of the heavens where the Azores highs form to provide Europe with fine weather.

The places people travel today! "I will never take another trip," you said to me a few days ago—you, who have sailed the seas so often. I was shocked, for I enjoy traveling. Now I'm glad I hid my disappointment, because my African village comes to mind.

It was before I started going to kindergarten. Someone had given me a sheet of cardboard with an African village on it, one of those sheets that you could get for only a few cents. When everything was all cut out and pasted together, there were some round cardboard huts, some native figures to set up, and perhaps a palm tree as well—I can't recall exactly. What I do remember is that I spent days alone in my room, squatting on the floor, playing with the huts. Undoubtedly I was already engaged in silent conversation—I wonder with whom.

If anyone had told me then that I had to take a trip to Africa, I would have found it most annoying to leave my beloved native huts, and I would also have probably been greatly confused, for I *was* in Africa.

Later there came a time when I could not get enough traveling. Of course it would be grotesque to compare the artistic merit of the pyramids of Giza and the temples of Bali to my African village, and of course one's life is richer for getting to know the world. But I am not sure whether I was happier amid the pyramids of Giza and the temples of Bali or whether I experienced more there than with my cardboard village. One thing is certain: My native huts impressed me at that time as being just as beautiful as the seven wonders of the world did later.

I like what Matisse said: Flowers bloom everywhere for anyone who has eyes to see them. A piece of cardboard and Africa is *there*—is that not inexhaustible riches? Is it perhaps that children and older people do not need to travel simply because they have the gift of fantasy? Now it does not strike me as a loss that you don't want to visit distant lands, but a strong, mysterious sense of self-repose. Children and wise men do not rush and do not travel —are they perhaps more intimately associated with creation? Whoever has deep roots in creation need not fly and travel far.

Scrap

Bernard's letter began so innocently: the business trip to Mexico, the hoop of gold he purchased hastily for his wife between two sessions, the increased turnover of the pharmaceutical products made by his division of the company. I read it all to you unsuspecting until I came to that sentence: "And then I'll be retired and tossed on the scrap heap." From the exclamation this sentence elicited from you, I was set for a vehement contradiction, and could not understand why you jumped up without a word and ran out of the room. How could I have guessed that the sentence was nothing more than your cue to empty our garbage can!

Now I'm standing alone in the kitchen with that sentence of Bernard's, while you shamble down the steps. You're not brooding over the charge, which probably seems to you mere foolishness. But his words have made me sad, because I know that they really do hold true for him, who was once my cheerful playmate. He almost makes a fool of himself trying to delay the terrible day of retirement a little, although he knows that in a huge company like his, his successor is already waiting impatiently behind his chair. That's how quickly a man is worn out and replaced in the business world of today! For more than four decades what mattered to Bernard was not the full utilization of his life but the accomplishment of work, and this inordinate need to be productive lasted from the day he came of age until his sixty-fifth birthday, from morning to evening or into the night—stifled his life and made him forget that he was worth so much more than his position. His remorseless activity choked off his openness to art, to nature, to people, perhaps even to God. For all love needs time—love of God, love of men, and love of things. And he has had time only for things. Will he discover his own dignity once more, sense himself as a creature of God, or like a workhorse put out to pasture, merely stand in dread of the gift the creator offers him once more, the gift of life?

Ashes

You sit there holding your newspaper, but you're not reading. One leg dangling over the armrest, your head propped up—your favorite position in your chair.

Perhaps you've forgotten that I'm standing behind you dusting the library. Once again I'm gathering dust in a cloth, to shake it out somewhere else while the new dust is already gathering. But since I stopped being irritated by this pointless charade, it gives me occasion to reflect; that is my small triumph over this law of nature that seeks to enslave me for life.

When I met you I was once more collecting books—although after the war, when my library had turned to ashes, I didn't want to buy any more books, not a single one. Now they fill a whole wall once more. We both kept an eye out for rare editions or ancient volumes; but at times I have the feeling that you are only playing with me, that you do not want to spoil my fun when I discover a new treasure, although you don't take the matter seriously. You play attentively and patiently with children, too; you'll hunt high and low for a doll or a train for them; you're even happy to play with them yourself. But you're always aware that it's only a game, and you wouldn't care if someone came and kicked over the doll's house or smashed the little train. You'd only be sorry on account of the children. It's hard for you to hide what you're thinking, and yet you sometimes keep things well concealed even from me, perhaps only so as not to disappoint me. You love your chair, I suppose, because you can dream in it, rather than because it is a work of art.

I know that after the war, when you were repatriated from Japan, you were not unhappy in a room that was furnished in terrible taste; one gets used to ugliness and ceases to see it, you explained to me. But for my part, ugliness will always gall me, and my shabby excuse is that ugliness is merely a human artifact. In nature no ugliness offends me, but we no longer live in natural surroundings. We live in houses, between walls, where one cannot plant a tree or conjure up a mountain, and there I yearn for the beautiful small things shaped by human hands, although I know that they are ballast and a spark can devour them once more, as in the war.

You sit there with your newspaper, but you are not reading.

What if we both were to toss the contents of our life into a giant sieve today—how much would be ashes, sifting through the mesh; how much would remain behind, for us to hold in our hands?

I touch you lightly as I pass, out of tenderness. Is it because I am glad that you are alive, that I am alive, and that we met? Merely a gesture of thanks. And because I am happy to sense that if everything we have collected were to turn once more to ashes and fall through the sieve, we should still be fortunate to have each other.

Distribution

I brush the spines of our books with my bright feather duster, almost caressing rather than cleaning—playacting, not dusting! Perhaps it was as a substitute for my career in the theater, from which I was wrenched by the postwar period and then our marriage, that I raised the level of housekeeping a little and made it an extension of the theater. I still take delight in the chambermaids, today considered so hackneyed, who played so flirtatiously and foolishly with a feather duster while talking so cleverly. You confirmed my dilettantish approach to housekeeping when our first venture into entertaining proved a total disaster, and you had to race to the nearest delicatessen to give our guests enough to eat, and I was on the verge of despair. Then you comforted me by saying, "Just don't turn into the perfect housewife!" What music to my heart!

Perhaps you were not thinking of the perfect housewife whose kitchen looks like a sparkling laboratory and whose children sleep tidily in their beds, while she looks like a model receiving twelve guests for dinner. Such perfect housewives really do exist, and for me they will always remain one of the wonders of the world. You, of course, were thinking of that unperfect perfect housewife who can certainly present a perfect household—in the midst of which one is beaten down by washing and dusting and polishing and groaning.

Even though our guests now get enough to eat, I shall never be a perfect housewife, perfect or unperfect, but I am firmly convinced that you would not be really happy with either: the former would stifle you, the latter would put you to flight. Because our household works by improvisation, you enjoy jumping in whenever you feel like it—going shopping, cooking, even carrying out the garbage. I never asked you to do it; you have just carried out the garbage pail ever since I can remember, as a natural gesture of consideration, and you usually carry it off singing. The men regard you on the steps with disapproval, perhaps because of their guilty consciences or because they expect you at least to wear a sullen expression. Of course, you don't always jump in just when it would help me most with the household work— then you may be dreaming or listening to music. But to press you at those moments would curtail your freedom. In our informality you feel unconstrained and I feel superior in my accommodation —that seems to me an agreeable distribution.

Something Different

You asked me why Verena called. That a woman may call up without a particular reason is beyond your comprehension. For you the telephone was an irksome instrument belonging to your work and its ringing a tyrannical imperative, so that you now take a kind of satisfaction, perhaps as an act of revenge, in letting it ring without obeying its command. But it gets under my skin, and when the tyrant calls three times without your stirring, I run to answer.

What could I have told you about my telephone conversation with Verena? She hoped it would get cooler. A few days ago she wanted warmth. Tomorrow she will long for rain because her garden is so dry, and the next day for sun because she is afraid that it will mildew. Strange how people always want something different, not only from the weather, but from the stock market, from business, from politics; and of course "different" means better. But what is really better, the great difference that comes with death—that they do not wish for. That makes them afraid.

Letters

You brought me the notice with its brutal black border. You were fond of her, this last of your mother's friends. Now you are searching for words of comfort for her three daughters. I wonder whether the word "God" will be in your letter.

In letters of joy when a child is born or a couple is married, we easily make do without this word. Life is opening out before the people we are writing to, a life that—all experience notwith-standing—appears without end, and the word does not need to be mentioned. Our letters radiate strength and happiness even without it. But in the presence of death, if one cannot lean on Him, the world suddenly totters and it is impossible to find the most meager morsel of comfort for the survivors.

Why do we, you and I, write the word so rarely, and why do we speak it so hesitantly? Is it perhaps because He is sometimes oppressively near and sometimes terrifyingly distant? How can I tell whether now, at this very moment, you sense that He is almost touching, or whether you feel separated from Him by a gulf? At times when God is distant, no one should talk to me about the word; I need all my strength to keep from losing it, for I can never possess it, only be possessed by it. My distance from God is incalculable; it rarely terrifies me when He lays burdens upon me, it sometimes torments me when I see others suffer whom I love, or it creeps in when I am carefree—I never know when it will come.

Should we speak of Him whom we cannot comprehend with our senses, who sweeps away our reason until we have only faith left to hold fast to? Should we fall silent concerning Him? The word is not often spoken between us, but we know in our silence that it bears us up.

Riddles

Through our kitchen window I can see you talking without hearing you, as in an old silent comedy. A while back the professor would not have stopped you on the street and involved you in a lengthy conversation. But now, since he has had to turn over his laboratory at the factory to a young scientist, he suddenly has lots of time. You stand there, impatiently shifting the bag with the groceries for our lunch, and I have to turn the broiler off again until you have extricated yourself from the conversation. Perhaps he's explaining to you something you have no desire at all to know —that the insecticide residues on the apples you're bringing home can be precisely determined and controlled by thin-film chromatography, for that was his field of research. A tiny field in one of the many sciences, and his successor will undoubtedly find still more accurate methods.

My field of study makes me covetous of the knowledge that will always be a closed book to me. I would love to understand the laws of physics, of astronomy, of paleontology—a goal for which my thought and my life in this world will not suffice. How exciting I find the conclusions of scientific study that do come within my ken—ideas about the development of the universe and the mutation of mankind, ideas that will remain a mystery to me on this earth. I do not know which would fascinate me more: the structure of a tiny (to me, a human being) atom or the structure of our gigantic (to me, a human being) solar system, which in turn is as tiny as an atom within the universe. How relative our knowledge is! But this relativity must not drive us into an attitude of resignation; we are, after all, to "subdue the earth"! Relativity should lead us to the one invisible creator of order, like the astronaut who took bread and wine along and celebrated the Lord's Supper on the moon, on the first heavenly body ever trod by a man of earth—among innumerable billions of other heavenly bodies. The loneliest Supper of a man—knowledge resting in faith.

Perhaps in that other realm of God, in our other form of

existence, we—you and I, the wise and the foolish, the scholars and the public—will understand the meaning of the universe, eternity, infinity. But here, upon this earth, does not he who loses himself in God gain more than he could ever find in scientific knowledge?

For Pennies

When I spied the rotten apple in the sack, why did I pick it out instead of ignoring it? No, you came back happy from buying the groceries. You showed off your purchases to me so proudly—not noticing, of course, that the salesgirl, undoubtedly with a smile, had stuck a wormy apple into your bag in the store—and the money wasted really doesn't matter a bit; nevertheless, I pulled out the apple like a reproach and spoiled your pleasure for no reason. How much easier it is to meditate on billions of heavenly bodies than to control the tiniest harmful inclination!

The Old Battle

I set the table carefully with the green linen cloth and the red plates, and you don't see it. You don't taste the steak you broiled so perfectly, don't notice the rose, your favorite flower, that I set between us, whose perfume flirts so infatuatingly with you. You are livid with rage. If only the phone call had come later, after our dinner, which was meant to be a feast.

You were never able to put up with injustice and fought against it at work whenever it came within your sphere. Your impassioned intervention was often futile, but in the heat of battle you were able to transform your anger into activity. Now you are forced to hear about a man being passed over so that someone less competent, who enjoys the protection of someone or other, can be promoted. I had not realized that being forced to look on without doing anything would be a more bitter blow to you than even hopeless intervention.

Today as always men everywhere groan under the injustice that asserts itself by force of position, of wealth, of arms. Not just back then in some dark ages, but today. And it will be no different tomorrow. But that, I think, is not what matters. Neither is it what matters today, nor did it matter in the time of Jesus.

What did Jesus do in his world of exploitation, of war, of oppression? He did not consider that injustice was the crucial factor, but God. He knew that there were plenty of poor, but he did not lead a campaign against poverty—"the poor you have always with you"!—because that, compared to his campaign for God, was probably secondary. Nor did Jesus lead a campaign against the rich; he feared only that their wealth could separate them from God. He even loved the rich young man. Jesus healed the centurion's servant without requiring that the centurion quit his military service, but rejoiced instead in the faith that he found in this officer. Jesus entered the house of the tax collector and did not command him to give up his profession, but required only that he exact no more than was just. To be rich or to be poor, to do military service or to refuse military service, to have a respected profession or a despised profession—such things were secondary to him. All that mattered was God. And love for God made it *obvious* for a rich man to help a poor man, for a centurion to be concerned about one of his soldiers, for a tax collector not to profiteer; made it obvious that one should simply love one's neighbor. For though it is possible not to believe in God and yet take thought for one's fellowmen, it is impossible to love God and disdain one's fellowmen. God is always primary; the good of the state, social principles, vocation, are secondary.

If we place our faith primarily or exclusively in human progress and in a world of freedom and justice here on earth, we shall sooner or later be shattered by disappointment. We can help build a relatively more cooperative world, nothing more. Today, as always, what revolutionizes the world is not humanism, not socialism, not any ism that will ever be; what revolutionizes the world is God and nothing else. We have no call to smile at Münchhausen: today more than ever we believe that we can use science and social justice to pull ourselves out of the quagmire by our own hair!

I love you because in your own small domain you always fought for justice. It will be important for you to find yourself a new, modest circle in which you can continue to work for justice—in the social realm, in the church, somewhere. For of course the battle for justice must continue to be fought throughout the world; without this continual battle on the part of all men of goodwill, even if it can never lead to total victory, injustice would gain the upper hand. But whether justice is done or not is not the ultimate, crucial concern.

NOON

Doing Nothing

Silence. The middle of the day. You in your room, I in mine. I wonder what you are doing. Perhaps nothing at all? How often have you told me how as a child in Alexandria you used to lie on the roof of your house looking at the sky, following a cloud until it dissipated. Sometimes you bring me along into the charmed circle of quiet. You are a master of that idleness in which no boredom lurks, no inertia threatens; you know how to just *be* there, with no special purpose, actively resting. This calm strikes me as a pause for breath within creation, a silent, invisible, imponderable movement—happy hours of inactivity in which the soul can operate. Rest without God—how oppressive it must be! Rest in the presence of God—the bliss it brings!

Results

I hear you hammering away at your typewriter in your room. When you are so carried away by your typing you are undoubtedly working on your memoirs. You used to be able to work on them now and then on Sunday afternoons, but now the days of the week no longer have names for us, and the hours of the day have no numbers, and you can write whenever you feel so inclined! Soon you will rush in, bearing the new page victoriously in hand, read it happily to me, and look at me expectantly. On the last page you described your doctor's waiting room in Alexandria, where you waited suspiciously—a small boy in a sailor suit, sitting up stiffly—and played with the tassels of the overstuffed chair; the green tassels, long turned to dust, which I never saw, sway before my eyes, silly and pointless. I am enchanted by your accounts of Egypt as it was. But now I am worried—worried that at the conclusion of this job in which you can immerse yourself now you might be disappointed because, although it delights the two of us, it may not find a responsive audience elsewhere.

Actually I shouldn't worry, for it probably does not really matter whether you are working with colors, words, or music, clay or gold, silk or cotton, whether you are shaping a knickknack or a masterpiece. Your efforts—that is what seems to me to be important, because we grow through our efforts. As we shape a thing, we form ourselves. If God grants us talents that differ, some outstanding, some modest, do our efforts not matter more to Him than the results?

A Blind Man

How you raced down the two flights of stairs when you saw the blind man hesitate, looking for the entrance! The workmen who have torn up the sidewalk are spending their noon hour somewhere in the shade, and there is no one on the street. We don't even know the blind man's name, but for years we've seen him on holidays, when we're at home, always taking the same route to the apartment. His step is sure with his tapping cane, he is equally friendly to all who speak to him, and we admire him.

Now you've reached him and are walking beside him. A minor event. But is life not more a series of small helpful acts than a single great action? You like people—you don't look past them; you listen to them. How easily the noise and bustle of daily life drown out the messages of our fellowmen; one must pay close attention to see and hear the needs of one's neighbors as they pass. Pay close attention, without seeking to invade men's privacy, so as not to pass by blindly on the other side when they are in silent distress.

How little attention we pay today to our fellowmen, hastening by with our own cares, our own work, our own ambition. We have grown in intelligence since we lived in caves, grown in knowledge; our brains have increased in size, but what about our hearts? In organized socialism, in collecting money for foreign nations in distant lands, we show ourselves very capable, and that is good; but it sometimes seems to me that we fail to see the men who cross our path in daily life. Jesus helped those who were near him: the woman who touched the hem of his garment, the blind man who sat by the wayside, the man in the mulberry tree. With our great projects in far-off lands, do we not sometimes forget small acts of help close by? Do we not perhaps pass someone by who has touched the hem of our garment in his need, someone who would pour out his heart to us? How else could there be more than twelve thousand suicides in a single year in our country? More than twelve thousand, and that does not include unsuccessful attempts. A terrifying number. How many of these people needed perhaps only someone who would listen to them and try to heed and help them? Paying heed to others—nothing more, no great sacrifice, but it can spell salvation.

The Gift of Retirement 33

A Song

You're coming back singing. If you meet a stranger on the stairs, he will stare at you suspiciously. Why are others so rarely happy to hear someone sing, even when they don't know what is making him happy? It sometimes seems to me as though the man who sings is accused of degrading the human achievement, for the proper conduct is to groan under this burden in order to demonstrate to others how weighty it is.

How resentfully the people on the street turn and look when you sometimes greet me with an aria at the door! And even here in the apartment we were at first met with suspicion because singing frequently resounded from our dwelling, until the neighbors came to realize that they could rely on your word and your help—although, and not because, you sing! In the civic chorus once a week between eight and ten, or at church on Sunday between ten and eleven, at fixed times and in the company of others, that is when they would have you sing, as befits a serious-minded employee.

To sing when one has experienced disappointments, war, disease; when one senses the steady approach of death; in the winter when the birds are silent—to sing at the moment and despite the moment—to free oneself from oneself in song!

I recall that my grandmother sang quite off pitch; but when we used to go up to our cabin in the mountains every summer, the donkeys trotting behind us with our supplies, and when we crossed the timberline at the final bend in the way, where we could look down upon the meadows like velvet below our feet and look up to see the crags towering above us—then she would simply break out singing even though she didn't really know how; she would sing out of tune in her tiny, soft voice, and we did not laugh at her. It was as though her soul were singing.

Our Time

How you are beaming because the woman at the newsstand remarked on your not being at work today. She thought you were much too young to be retired. People often think me, too, younger than I am, and it makes me as happy as it makes you. Again and again this harmless, helpless self-deception! For it does not make us younger to look younger, at best a little less threadbare outwardly! Is it not the time we bear within us that determines our age, not its outward marks upon us?

"In my time . . ." I can still recall how startled I was the first time this phrase escaped my lips, for I had always found it boring in the mouths of the elderly and a bit ridiculous when they boasted of it. When the words escaped me, the younger people at once spoke disdainfully and accusingly: Your time—dictatorship, war, injustice! Something was wrong here, and I suddenly felt called to the barricades to defend my time. That the generation before me was better off "in their time," in education, in art, in politics—these people are usually convinced of that. My generation has grown more cautious, for we know that things were worse then than they are today, back in the days when people lived caught between constraint and terror. And yet this time was "my time," and I was driven to justify it before the generation following me; I felt unsuspected tenderness toward it and wanted to defend it—not, of course, the crimes it held, but some-

The Gift of Retirement 35

thing that belonged to me and separated me from the following generation however much I might make the effort to bridge the gap. "My time" now seemed to me like a spoiled child that nevertheless remains my child and in whom I shall always find something good and lovely.

"In my time . . ." What does the phrase mean? At first I felt distressed that this could come between us like a foreign body, that I—differing in age by less than fifteen years!—would never be able to experience what your time was like, when the royal family was still the unimpeachable model of your childhood. But it seems to me that "my time" is less a specific segment of history than how we were formed by this segment, how we relate to this segment, and therefore for my generation "my time" means more—despite what the next generation thinks—than injustice, war, and violence.

To single out only a fragment: "My time" does indeed mean forbidden art, but it also means visits to studios where this art grows secretly in attics reached through backyards and back steps, and where the forbidden artist silently places picture after picture before us, not sensing that in our intoxicated hunger for this blazing statement we are not yet sated, and one of us says softly, "Slower!" . . . It means an air raid, then the arduous path through fields of ruins that smell of cold smoke, where in the undifferentiated mass of rubble one searches in vain for something recognizable, as in the monotony of the desert; then suddenly, on the spot where one seems to recall that a friend's house stood yesterday, a scrap of cardboard appears under a stone, with the familiar handwriting: "We are all alive." . . . No visit to a museum, where I can pay the admission fee and enter without dread; no visit to friends where I can simply ring the bell, and knowing that they are there can awaken such rejoicing in me.

"My time" definitely means more than a phase of foreign or domestic politics or a certain social upheaval; what is crucial is not the outward facts of history in that period but how I experienced my time, what I accepted and what I rejected in it. And so this time, however deeply it may bear the stamp of injustice and horror, I may tenderly call "my time."

And now the remarkable thing happens: now for you and me begins *our* time. A new gift of retirement! No longer separated by work in our daily lives, we shall both experience the same events. Today almost the entire day passes with us side by side, and yet each of us, you and I, will draw and preserve something different from it, something that will then go to make up *our* time. Just as a hundred painters see the same tree a hundred different ways, so your interior landscape will remain different from mine, and each will remain our separate secret; but each of these inner landscapes will be "right," just as each of the hundred different pictures of the same tree is "right." I do not know what you will make of this outwardly uneventful day, and I shall never find out what you will take out of future days with many events, but one thing I do know: you will never preserve and enjoy anything that today or in the future is unjust or evil. In you, therefore, I find strength, security, and confidence.

The Needles

However I pull it or tug it, the collar puckers; my alteration of this jacket is a failure. Could I hold the corner of the collar down with a stitch, using a very fine needle? Sewing needles! It is possible to love a man before one knows him well, but esteem grows only through a series of small things by which he unconsciously reveals himself; such a small thing was your sewing needles.

How light our baggage was when we assembled our belongings as a married couple after the war—your few suitcases, my odds and ends of furniture! The only heavy item was one of your suitcases, and I was curious about what it might contain. I was all the more astounded when I opened it and saw nothing but old mason jars—and why mason jars?—filled with packets of needles. I had no idea how heavy needles were en masse! The well-meaning man who, at the time of your repatriation from Japan, had forced upon you this treasure, for which there was obviously a secret source in the land of the cherry blossoms, thinking it would be valuable for barter in a starving Germany, had little knowledge of human nature. You had given away lots of them, bartered none, and finally forgotten them. Now they were worthless, since there was once again a stable currency, and I dumped them in the garbage.

I know there are many who would shrug their shoulders pityingly over you. It seemed to me that this indifference toward looking out for yourself, this cool disdain for your own advantage, gave you a remarkable strength in comparison with others in the postwar period—those who were forever hoarding, trading, longing for loot, even when the scramble for one's daily bread had long been a thing of the past. In the course of my life I have grown more and more suspicious of those who are good at their jobs and efficient at housework; they are a bit strange in their self-assured security. The ever so comfortable criteria of success, of profit, of reputation! Have we, you and I, always judged our co-workers and neighbors objectively, uninfluenced by outward signs of success and ability?

I think we should be careful with judgments—do we know the criteria by which He will one day judge us?

A Beaver Coat

Naturally a single glance was enough for you to see that the collar of my jacket puckers. How cleverly you pinned the brooch on the revealing spot! Now the defect is concealed, and with it (almost) the date of the style. And how much fun we had laying out the pattern! I think you would have been a good fashion designer—you can see at a glance what looks flattering on a woman. Would a fashion boutique perhaps have made our fortune? No, I much prefer having you pick out clothes only for me, not for others as well!

If you were rich, even an enormous closet would not suffice for all the dresses, purses, and shoes that you would bring me. Now you want to buy me the beaver coat you liked so much in the window. Ever since the furrier said that I wouldn't be able to wear it out in thirty years, I have suspected that I won't be able to restrain you, even though it destroys our budget. The thirty years settled it for you.

Your mind has always focused on the idea of making me secure in my old age: a dwelling of my own from which no one can evict me, a pension paid regularly, boots that I could walk halfway around the world in, and now a coat in which I can never freeze, which will last for many years. When I consider these thirty years I can only think of the last two wars, when everything that was secure suddenly turned insecure. You, too, went through this, but you refuse to see it, because some deep primitive fear makes everyone who loves want to protect the one he loves, precisely because he senses that preservation is beyond his power. Security we shall never find, not anywhere. How could you protect me from disaster, disease, war! Nor will any beaver coat help me if, just when I need it in an emergency, it is hanging in a closet I can no longer reach. Instead of security we must seek for confidence, and confidently shake off our fears.

Other People's Gardens

There you stand on our balcony, looking down at me. How comfortably you stand between the flower boxes! Undoubtedly you'll wait until my bus comes, watch how I get in, and wave to me once more. Now you're inspecting our geraniums, which flourish year in and year out with a splendor that continually amazes us.

You loved your garden in Japan; you often speak of the rose pergola in it, and this flower has been your favorite ever since. In the garden of my childhood, a eucalyptus tree was my special friend. Perhaps it struck me as being less touchy than the mimosas, less authoritarian than the pines; it stood, growing crooked, at the end of the garden, exalted and yet inconspicuous. I often paid it a visit, with my little monkey following me from branch to branch, howling his disapproval—for he would never climb about in this tree; he preferred the pines. So unobtrusive was my arboreal friend in his faded colors and irregular growth that I cannot even recall his silhouette precisely; but he always enticed me to play beneath his solid trunk, like a refuge of dependability. A watercolor by Gramatté, which I often admired in his studio, taught me to see the flowers of my eucalyptus. How painters can open our eyes! Without this picture I should never have noticed how the hard capsules are forced open by such delicate blossoms, as though by a miracle.

You're pointing to our neighbor, who is giving the garden in front of her house another vigorous raking. You no longer have a garden of your own, only fond memories of one; but you like to look at other people's gardens, without envy.

Earning

The light is turning yellow. Don't I know this stooped woman rushing to get to the curb? Oh, yes, it's the widow of the stove dealer. She often checks on her branch office near the corner by our apartment. How old she looks! Ever since her husband died she's lived alone—no relatives, no friends. But she works; she labors doggedly at the business that her husband built up, by which he earned his living and through which she continues to rake in money, which she invests in Switzerland, in America, wherever it looks safe. She spends little, and will soon be eighty. Isn't it spooky, this piling up of money and acting as though one didn't realize that one must die soon and not be able to take a red cent along? This woman strikes me as the very incarnation of the senseless struggle to earn money, driven by the lash of a demon. Many may doubt that we may carry over the fruits of our spirit with us into another life, but no one doubts that we shall never take the fruits of our labor, money, beyond the grave.

In the past only the poor tormented themselves with work, because they had to; today the rich do so as well, because they want to. Once work was considered degrading; now it earns respect. Strange—the ancient curse of the Bible that we should earn our bread by the sweat of our brow as punishment for our sins has been transformed by modern man, almost slyly, into a source of satisfaction, as though man to spite his creator undertook to do gladly of his own free will what he is cursed to do. But God will not be deceived, and this stratagem will not make men happy.

At some time in the past men began to ennoble work. When? My caveman who painted that wild horse had a sense of proportion: he hunted a bison when he felt hungry; it would have been senseless to slaughter more bison, whole hecatombs of bison, whose flesh would merely rot. It began with the first herd: a man might maintain one animal, ten, a hundred—there ceased to be any upper limit. A man might stake out ever larger fields and take possession of ever more land, and a small factory might grow into a larger one and sprout branches and finally produce a corporation. Undoubtedly man was driven into maintaining flocks, fields, and factories so as not to starve, and he solved his problem magnificently; but the setting of an upper limit, the keeping of a sense of proportion—for that man lacked the strength of self-control and self-respect. Earning money in a developed economy became the demon that drives us senselessly, debasing our lives until nothing remains but the function of eating and laboring. We have lost the rhythm of work and leisure. We have won ourselves one more day of rest in the week than God commanded, but into this day of rest we bring the restlessness our standard of living demands, a standard raised higher and higher by our making more and more money. The demon of making money will laugh us to scorn as he lashes us through a third holiday, that we may find no rest.

And we do not resist the demon; quite the contrary, we have made him our idol, just like the idolaters we smile at, for whether a golden calf is placed upon an altar or stored in a bank vault makes no difference. We find it a fit memorial to say of the departed that his work was his life. This depresses me. If a man's life was really nothing but work, he was a poor man, for only rarely did the departed do the work of a doctor or an artist or another one of the favored few whose labor can contain a blessing; usually he tormented himself with some dull activity of hand or brain merely in order to make money.

You still feel work to be degrading. How pleased you were yesterday at the statement of Ortega y Gasset that the nineteenth century stinks from one end to the other of the sweat of the working day! This does not mean that work itself is senseless. I always appreciated what my grandfather said, that all work worth doing is worth doing well. The smallest article, cleanly formed, radiates something good, I think. Working to make money—that is necessary to stay alive; making money to spend money—what tremendous pleasure that can bring! And you happily poured forth as much as you earned to give yourself and others pleasure. But one tiny step further, and one is trapped in the vicious circle of making money in order to make money.

What a new adventure retirement is! You have been able to break the curse of having to earn a living and now you are free, not only on evenings and weekends, but totally free to enjoy life and fill this day with whatever seems good to you and gives you pleasure: to do magic tricks like a fool, to do nothing like a philosopher, to help others like one who loves people, to dream like someone searching for God.

The Sword

Now, as I hurry along the street in order to be with you sooner, I am struck by the "thunder word." It always happens the same way: A Bible passage or a hymn verse will lie buried under the debris of years and then suddenly strike me, and the simple words are so powerful that I wince before them, like just now, in the middle of the street. Why is the thunder word resounding in my ears? Because I happened to cross paths with Margot, and she practically begged me to invite her and Edward tomorrow? He doesn't know how he will kill the time—kill is what she said—since their trip has been delayed for a day and they have nothing scheduled tomorrow.

Edward has too much time, I have too little time, and you simply have time, neither too much nor too little. But all three of us have the same time: eternity.

Eternity—that thunder word from the old hymn. Old-fashioned, very old-fashioned, centuries old, are the words of the hymn; but the fear in the words "my tongue doth cleave to my mouth"—that is not old-fashioned, that is today what agitates Edward and millions of others. And who could invent a better, more concise line: "O sword, that pierces through the soul"?

If a sword should pierce my body I would soon bleed to death, but with a sword in my soul I can survive for a long time, perhaps forever. Trying eternally to withdraw the sword that tortures me?

We can neither kill time nor beguile it, but we can fill it, for time is really whatever *I* make it. If I am surrounded by eternity, now while I am on the way home to you and always, and if in this portion of eternity, during my time on earth and later in whatever form God wills, I ripen and grow according to the creative plan of God, with my joy, my pain, my love, then I no longer feel a sword in my soul, only confidence.

Why am I hurrying home to you? To save a few seconds when there is all eternity? It is enough for me to use the time, this portion of eternity granted me on earth, to fill it meaningfully with whatever appears most urgent at any given moment, and to do so calmly, without hurry. Jesus had only three years for his ministry, and he set his stamp on billions of men. I should have confidence that God will give to us men on earth sufficient time to accomplish what we are intended to accomplish.

But now I still find myself running up the stairs to our apartment! I am running because I rejoice in being able to fill my time with *you* now. You are standing in the doorway; you have seen me coming. You are smiling. Eternity is our time.

EVENING

Scope

You have made tea for me in your room. I drink it gratefully, swallow by swallow. I'm always freezing when I come back from seeing my sick mother. Today her body, which once moved so gracefully in elegant clothing, seemed chained even tighter to her wheelchair, and all that is left of her scintillating spirit is this sadly smiling, questioning glance. How good it is that in our youth, when we demolish authorities, we do not notice how little scope we have for our small liberties between sickness and death! Unrestricted freedom is ours only in one thing: the freedom to love.

The Guest

The tea is growing cold in our cups. There is silence between us. Now I should really tell you that I have invited Margot and Edward to come over tomorrow evening, and that I couldn't check with you in advance. You will flare up, because you don't like him; on that point it is difficult to bargain with you. I will postpone the news a bit, remain silent for several moments.

Are the two of them at home already? Perhaps at this very moment she is also drinking tea with him. But he is getting impatient. I can see it: he crushes out his cigarette, jumps up, walks up and down in the room, and Margot looks anxiously after him. He takes another cigarette out of his pack, lights it with trembling hand. Always the same game. The luxuriant garden at his feet—

he's bored with it. The rare books in the library around him—he's weary of them. Ever since retirement he's been fleeing from himself, from his own emptiness which had been concealed by his busy job and which he suddenly found himself thrust into. He flees from country to country, from room to room. And if he and Margot are alone in a room, thrown back upon themselves, they can find no word or thought of joy for each other after a life together that never went beyond "doing things" and giving presents. Boredom stalks him everywhere and pursues him. To escape the threat he seeks out clubs, people, trips, transforming the quiet of retirement into hectic activity. As an addict cannot live without morphine, he needs the poison of activity, for he can still get about. But let him once be chained to a sickbed, and he will suffocate. Perhaps he suspects the truth, and fear stands between him and Margot.

Boredom—what does that mean? Things and people cannot produce boredom, for no one and nothing can compel me to be bored. Is it a kind of self-disgust, when the pleasure never comes that one has promised oneself, because one has sought in things what they in their transitoriness could not give, and one now finds everything insipid? Between you and me, now, in our silence, there is no boredom, but simply joy. Why? Because God is present? Because we make room for Him as for a guest who is always expected? Does boredom creep in when people keep God out? Is boredom separation from God? I do not know. Works by doctors and psychologists, by poets and monks, have not given me a clear answer. But one thing I know: day by day we must fight to keep the room free for the guest who brings joy; for where joy is, there is no room for boredom.

The Photo Album

We must interrupt our teatime. I should clear away the dishes and go to my room, but I am held as though by a spell.

I wonder what you are thinking about as you get the photo album. When you open it, it is full of people I do not know, with whom you converse in silence. With what fascination you get the album out from time to time! The Japanese silk of its cover is already quite tattered. Although I know scarcely any of them, all the faces on the fading pictures are familiar to me, so often have you shown them to me. This album contains your life before we met, almost half a century, and most of the people who stare out at us are already dead, your father amid the bombs, your mother of starvation. I would have loved to thank your parents for everything they were to you, and I never knew them. Your friends, comrades, fellow workers went to an early death; two world wars have reduced your generation to tatters, like the silk of the cover.

The Egyptian pictures strike me today as being a bit more blurred: you and your classmates on a donkey expedition through the desert; you with your four sisters, all in white sailor suits, at the German school in Alexandria, enthusiastically waving little flags to greet the German crown prince and his wife. Now come the photos that are clearer, their outlines hardly faded: you as a soldier, seventeen years old—the uniform flaps about your under-nourished body, standing stiff before the photographer as on the parade ground; you in Kobe, now very relaxed, between two dis-creetly smiling Japanese girls at a party; you in front of the devas-tation of an earthquake—vanished history, buried men.

Soon you will be wearing your strange smile, as though you noticed something that I cannot see. The word "death" will not be spoken between us, but it will be written between the pictures, stand behind us in the room. Now you are getting our photo album, the one with our eleven years of marriage! It still looks new, and has a stout leather cover. Now, as you turn the pages, are you thinking that one of us will be left behind? One of us will someday turn the pages without the other, and run his fingers silently over the face of his beloved.

But today we are alive, you and I, and a new time is beginning: the two of us are free for each other and for what we love. Close the album with its many faces that no longer exist— I love being alive with you! I am happy and can do nothing to delay aging and death, but for us aging must not be merely a humiliating bodily decay. Aging is our exaltation, our spiritual growth toward God, in expectation and joy.

Talents

Betty has interrupted our silence. She always comes at an awkward time, but she never notices, and so we can't hold it against her. You gave me a meaningful look when she told how she had found a talented young architect whom she wanted soon to see about remodeling her summer house. The summer house as a rendezvous for lonely women who once were busy at their jobs: a good idea—who worries about these uncomplaining souls? —but it will always be "soon," for she has had this idea for many years, and the wild grapes still overgrow her little summer house.

It's strange how people make plans. We know so many people living in retirement who intend to do so much. All the things they plan—to establish a club, to work for the Red Cross, to write a book—and what are they doing when we see them again, years later? They are still planning, and in the meanwhile they have been looking after themselves and their small pleasures, losing more and more of their joy. They play cards a little, take a little walk, read a little—a few pages from the latest best seller—talk with others a little, and appear, above all, concerned not to wear themselves out.

How easily we sink into indolence: we sleep a little longer, drink a little more, mindlessly let the sounds or pictures from the radio or television pass before us a little longer, exercise our intellects a little less—always just "a little"—and gradually we slip into a horrible aversion to all exertion, drifting off like a drowning man who no longer moves his arms and legs to save himself. The indolence that began so harmlessly ends in deathly lethargy.

Do these people know that they will never get beyond the stage of planning? But why do they continually speak of what they want to do and yet never accomplish? Are they unconsciously trying to justify themselves in their own eyes and the eyes of others, because they sense that they are letting what powers they still have wither instead of using them productively? If they were convinced that they should use their days rightly, they would have to admit that they are content to fill their lives with themselves, for no one else demands of them surrender of their well-earned rest.

Are these people who let their powers languish unused in indolence not like that man in the parable who, instead of working with the talent entrusted to him and using it to bring interest, buries it in the ground? They act as though the talent were not lent them by the one to whom they will someday have to render an account; they have separated themselves from the giver, made themselves their own lords, and now believe they are accountable to no one.

It strikes me that it is an act of disrespect toward God to take the wealth he gives and let it lie fallow instead of using it creatively. But how difficult it is to find the right degree of composure between hectic activity and laziness! There are many waiting for us, for you, for me, for everyone who has time and energy—crippled children, the elderly, released prisoners, exhausted mothers, bedridden invalids—all of whom need help. Will we have the strength to frame our plans according to our gifts, perhaps not ambitious plans, but plans that we will undertake at once to carry out as our strength permits, to carry out at once?

Only a Glance

The way you winked at me just now when Betty was talking about her summer house! When you give me that special look, I feel a flood of tenderness within me. I could simply tell you that I love your eyes the way I love your hands, the way I love everything about you, but it would not be true. What makes this tenderness well up within me is not the special appearance of your eyes or their blueness; it is what finds expression in them: love, forbearance, sympathy—your soul. Your soul, which I cannot see, although it captivates me. Neither can I see the force of gravity that binds me to the earth. So much that matters in this life is invisible: the force of gravity, the soul. God.

Joy

The Matisse book lies gleaming on my desk; you surprised me without saying a word.

You know that I love Matisse, who said of his painting that he meant it to be like an easy chair in which a tired man can find rest—together with a little happiness, a little luxury, a little pleasure. Matisse—a breath of joy, as someone said of him.

I hold your gift in my hand and I am happy. Not only because you bought me the book while I was visiting my mother, but because of the words you wrote inside it, which I looked for there on the very first page, where you are wont to toss an idea impulsively to me like a ball for me to catch. "We do not know, God, where You are, but we do know that You are."

Because the word is seldom spoken between us and has not been spoken aloud today, I receive it thankfully in your handwriting on our first happy day of retirement. For the unbeliever every joy is darkened by the shadow of total extinction; for the believer, joy unfolds in maturing toward God—happiness without shadow, without end.

The Ball

You tossed the ball to me: I thought I had caught the words you wrote for me in the Matisse book, but they eluded me, and I have to try to grasp them.

"We know that You are." Do you also speak to Him in silence? I never began consciously to speak to Him; it was natural for me from childhood on, ever since my parents gave me the Bible with illustrations from Rembrandt and I could see the pictures of what they read to me every evening. How important pictures are to children! Do grown-ups always realize that fact? Pictures are companions. The later process of freeing oneself from the familiar representations is painful, but this kind of training must be adopted, for I do not think that children can love without images. Can *we* ever fully do so?

I have always spoken with Him, at first simply and directly, since He had sent us Jesus and my parents had said that He was present, mysteriously invisible. Later I spoke more cautiously, more tentatively, exhausting myself with questioning; then I spoke more confidently once again. It could also happen that for long periods I had no words to say to Him, nothing of my own, only things that I learned by rote, because at the time He seemed very far away and unreachable. But he was never absent. He was present, just as you write.

Simply *present*? How dangerous that is to say! It brings to mind the wicked comment that I heard once in a conversation: "Oh, them—they have God sitting in the corner of the sofa." For a long time this statement frightened me, for I could not simply shrug it off; there was a kernel of truth in it. To let one's thoughts roam close to God, not with false grandeur, stilted language, solemn gestures, but also not casually—to turn to him attentively, carefully, composedly. I think that when one loves God false accents vanish.

The framework of our life is our turning in thought to Him, centering our lives on Him, even when we do not have our hands folded or an invocation in our mouths. It seems to me that praying does not differ fundamentally from sending one's thoughts to God, requesting, asking, thanking.

But whoever does not believe in Him, does he converse with Nothing? With Nothing I cannot engage in conversation. Does the unbeliever remain silent? How oppressively lonely my life would be without this constant silent dialogue with God! I am happy that you wrote these words in the book. God, who is present, turns this pivotal day, which many think marks the beginning of a descent, into an ascent and a day of joy for us.

Deliverance

The rush of wings in the room, a shadow above my head—the swift was undoubtedly more terrified than I was when he suddenly found himself caught in the lace of the curtains. How quickly you turned up the dustrag while I was still trying to think how to help the young bird, which was desperately beating with its wings at the folds of the curtain, and how dexterously you grasped its tiny body firmly and protectively under the soft material, carefully extricating its claws from the net with your other hand. With a swing of your arm you propelled the little creature through the open window, and it regained its freedom. Now you're looking after it, smiling.

At this very moment millions of creatures are in fear and agony, but it is nevertheless a source of happiness to relieve a single being, no matter how small, of its pain and fear.

Where We Go

What a new adventure awaits us in retirement: we can go wherever we like, no longer wherever we must. For the most part in this life we are pushed into one place or another, by our family, by our job; only rarely do we have free choice. Now we can simply choose the natural surroundings and a city that attract us, and we are looking forward to our retirement home as impatiently as children waiting for a tent at Christmas.

We were also as frivolous as children when we bought our house, because the view over the church tower with its heavy cupola and over the bright baroque palace between the dark pyramids of the thuja trees captivated us. We were delighted by the heavy wooden doors in the ancient building, which recalled the south of our childhood, by the balconies with their intricate wrought iron, by the staircase that winds playfully from floor to floor, an extravagant waste of space, a staircase up and down which one can float and which naturally made you decide on a polonaise for the dedication. It was love at first sight, and our purchase was decided the very second the two of us stepped out on the balcony of my room, the smiling city lying at our feet.

From our present concrete dwelling we view a horizon surrounded more by chimneys than by trees, and yet we hold on to this utilitarian apartment, because we have been happy here. In our new home, too, what matters will not be the beautiful view or the harmony between the rooms, but the happiness we bring with us.

The Rag Doll

You have put on *The Seasons* by Haydn, and I would rather not enter your room. I know that now you are listening to the music with an intensity that carries you far away from here. What a gift to be so easily enraptured! It is not only music that enraptures you—you can lose yourself completely in something quite insignificant. I wonder if you hear the inner music of things?

It is only a poor comparison, but I am reminded of my rag doll. In fact, it was not even my doll but my cousin's, probably acquired by chance from some little girl in our family, now grown up. In any case it lay among his toys, where he never deigned to give it even a glance. Its poor limbs, filled with sawdust, dangled uselessly; the eyes on its grotesquely flat face were faded. But I loved this doll, which did not belong to me, more than any of my expensive china ladies with their clinking eyes and long lashes, and whenever I visited my cousin I rushed to see the doll. Perhaps I loved it because it nestled like a living thing when one held it close, while my china dolls in their silken gowns remained cold and hard. When I held it blissfully to my breast, in all its ugliness, was I hearing the inner music of things? Today I have forgotten what my own dolls looked like, but this rag doll I can never forget. For me it was a source of music, and this music gives me pleasure even today.

I think that when we rest content in ourselves, as we can do unconsciously when we are children but must relearn by dint of conscious training when we are adults, then things begin to sound and we hear their music. We discover how rich we are, and everyday life becomes a festival.

Where They Go

You were silent at my news, and so I know that you are overwhelmed by a torrent of thoughts. Bernard, who always stormed into the administration building taking two steps at a time, who urged everyone to work faster, had told the driver to drive faster, and then came the accident. Ten years you fought him with memorandums that he swept off his desk and with suggestions that he ripped to shreds—the modern duel between two men that is not as bloody as the duel of the past with its weapons, but seems to me even more cruel. Now Bernard is crippled and eliminated. If only he had somehow dropped out earlier; for you it is ten years too late. What strength you need to draw on now to control your thoughts, to turn a raging torrent into a calm stream!

Day in, day out, thoughts of business, private matters, politics, nurture their source of energy, seething, invisible, inaudible, intangible, good or evil, not subject to restraint by force of man or arms. "Never speak of it, always think of it"—the French knew what power this admonition would engender after they lost the Franco-Prussian War. A man can be slain, but not a thought. How many thoughts do we conceive in a day? No computer can count them. How many fly like sparks from one man to another, to go out or to catch fire? We often speak of people talking at cross purposes, but is it not thinking at cross purposes that really matters?

I can restrain my words, not my thoughts. Only when a thought has suddenly burst forth within me can I engage my will, pursue it if it strikes me as being good, eschew it if it appears dangerous; but as soon as I cease consciously to suppress it, it springs forth again. My words are made visible to others in the form of letters, through writing; in the form of sound, through my voice; and the words that I have spoken or written can survive after my death. But the thoughts that I have had, for all, even for you, invisible, inaudible, good or evil, go with me to the grave. Or to God?

No one can prevent Him from perceiving our thoughts. An idea full of joy and terror: "God knows what you need before you ask him."

I do not know your thoughts, although we are one flesh. But one thing I do know: if my thoughts today had been filled with hatred or even with resentment toward you, they would have poisoned the day for both of us. The happiness of our marriage is borne by the feeling that we have friendly thoughts toward each other, even when they do not always turn into words that the other may hear. I do not know what you have been thinking today and what you are thinking now, but I know that your thoughts toward me are good, and that makes me strong and glad.

Otherwise . . .

I cannot forget that statement; it sums up the meaning of life. I read it years ago in a newspaper article, I've forgotten by whom. An old man is setting his affairs in order before his death, which he suspects is soon to come; he distributes his costly library, then interrupts himself suddenly, and while still making his preparations, says quite incidentally to the young friend who is helping him, "Of course, you believe in immortality; otherwise, nothing would have any meaning."

Otherwise your life, my life, and this happy day would have no meaning. Twelve words. Twelve thousand words could not say more.

At the Window Again

I caught the right moment once again: the bus has pulled up to the stop. Has it also drawn you to the window?

Now they are getting out, tired, taciturn. They have left—at least many of them—a good measure of their daily strength at their jobs. The professor's smile is subdued, the black curls of the girl who used to be a laborer are blown about, the chronometer man's watch remains in his pocket, and the former bachelor only makes a suggestion of lifting his hat. Only the secretary is, as always, unchanged, no hair out of place, no creases in her dress, uncannily self-contained.

Perhaps you feel a touch of melancholy after all? Even though you didn't love your job, you feel indebted to the company; it took you on after the war, when you were out of work—you always told me that on days of disappointment, and never forgot it.

Strange, this relationship with a giant that supported you and, barring catastrophes, will continue to support you to the end of your life. In return you have given the major portion of your strength. That is a tie, not like the tie that binds one to another person, but also not like the tie one feels toward an object. What does it mean to say "our company" (for we always say "our")? It is not the administration, the directors known individually by name; it is not the anonymous army of wage earners; it is more than the sum of men and jobs, of social institutions and cultural events; in a strange way it bears a personal stamp that distinguishes it from the other giants. Undoubtedly for you it is first and foremost the little host of workers whom you knew personally; it is this man and that man, this man who had the accident, who can no longer be chained to his desk, and that man who always knew how to send you, and all the others who could not get their suggestions accepted, away like conquerors, filled with renewed desire to accomplish other plans—you always left his room happy! But it is more to you than this small host of workers that you know out of the many thousands, whom you respected and encouraged or rejected and contended with; it is the soil on which you came to maturity in the struggle on behalf of or against others; it is "our company," with which you will remain intimately bound up.

The Journey

Retirement does not mean withdrawal but a challenge to a man. Now the final requirement is made of him: perseverance. Retirement is neither surrender nor resistance nor passivity, but the highest form of activity—not visible or directed outward, but inward. It is the state in which one begins to order one's baggage for an unsettling journey that brooks no comparison. Now begins the great process of selection, to take with us what is needful. We do not know the customs regulations, but we suspect that they will be strict, and that much will be taken from us when we cross the border: our baggage must hold much in little. A man spends an entire lifetime training himself, following his profession, and all only that he may assemble his equipment for this journey, piece by piece. Here and there things have been picked up, often without thought, as one may pick up something while passing a display, not even stopping to consider, because it suddenly seems to be just what is needed. Many things we have picked up will be useless, because in the daily harness we have thought too casually or too rarely of the journey. Now we have everything assembled and must sort it over; but now we also have leisure, for the first time, and now we must test, distinguish, reject—for who wants to set out on a journey with superfluous baggage! How often we have packed our bags, happily expectant, only to find out upon arrival in a distant land that we have brought the wrong things along and now must freeze in clothing that is too light or be hampered by pieces that are too heavy. What we shall take is clearly determined by our destination: whether we believe we are journeying to oblivion or to a new realm of God.

Loose Connection

It was a gift of chance that *The Magic Flute,* your favorite opera, was on television with a good cast on our first quiet evening. You were so happy that you would undoubtedly have joined in singing Tamino's portrait aria. I, too, was all anticipation as I turned down the lights for our gala presentation and as the director in the theater pressed a magic button for all to begin. That the set only crackled a bit, and then remained dark and silent was a trick played on us by technology. Of course, I shouldn't have uttered the words "loose connection" by way of excuse, but you know that this is my sole explanation for any failure of technology, of which I understand nothing, and at other times you laugh.

Today your disappointment was too great; instead of calming you, my words infuriated you, and you gave me a scathing look.

Alas, our daily lives have a diabolical way of hiding loose connections to plunge us from anticipation into disappointment. To overcome this fact will probably take unending discipline!

What shall I do? I cannot calm you with words, and yet I must tear you loose from the bitter brooding you have fallen into. Your room is no longer an opera house with dimmed lights and orchestra seats. Even if you tell me not to, I will turn out the lights and fling open the window. . . . Nothing beautiful finds its way in, only the corrosive atmosphere of the factory and the noise of the street. But now there takes place the small miracle that I sometimes experience in the course of the evening, which always unsettles me. Suddenly, as at a secret signal, silence descends; the sounds of the cars, of the lawn mowers, of the radios—everything pauses for a moment. You have come to the window behind me; you, too, are attentive. We listen. The noise of men is silent. The sound of the universe meets our ears. The music of God.

His Calling

Something I do almost every day: I light the candle in our old, bent pewter candlestick. During the evening it often burns on our table, between our books and newspapers. But now it seems to me as though the simple white candle lights us to a celebration.

What happened today? Almost nothing; you said hello to a couple of people, helped a blind man, bought a book, played a record. Almost nothing happened, and yet much: silently the two of us have grown richer. We will preserve our good thoughts and our good things, lighten our ballast, make ourselves trim and strong, that we may pass unburdened from this way of life to the next.

For this purpose we were granted something wonderful: today. We no longer say "then," but "now." This moment *now* is our treasure, not the next. With the tiny stirrings of the moment we grow quietly toward maturity, even if the strength of our bodies ebbs, for we shall lay aside this body at the final change in our way of life.

The desire that tempts us with illusions—a better job, greater success, more money—desire that is only a scourge and never fulfillment, we shall not regret. A "great day" we are unlikely to experience—it might easily be a lost day—but within us something much more powerful is stirring: we experience in the quiet hour that we are part and parcel of God's creative plan, not "then," but now. At this moment you stand before Him active, even if you have left the world of human labor. What does your work for the company amount to, measured against the tasks that may yet come your way today? You are an integral part of a process from which you can never be cut off. He who created you has need of you for the fulfillment of His work. What matters is not your position, your honors, your money—you yourself are required.

We must not seek contentment in "We have done it," or wallow in self-pity in "We have been written off," or think "We have escaped once more" when we have merely taken the easy way out, overlooking the fact that what is demanded is our involvement, not our comfort. No, we must present ourselves to today with the strengths and talents that are given us; then our day will be adapted to the ongoing work of God. No longer hired by men, but called by Him—how rich we are! Or is it presumptuous to believe that we are not useless, that we can cooperate in realizing the plan of creation? We always have some strength to offer, strength of body or of spirit, of experience or of kindness, and were we crippled or chained to our beds, we would surely have love to offer, gaiety and intercession. In His eyes we are never poor and never old. A source of annoyance? A burden? Hardly. When you are old and sick and in people's way and they push you aside, He who created you will snatch you up. To retire means to take up God's calling—what joy that we can experience it together, that we can help each other to grope our way to Him!

Our retirement is not a decline, but an ascent to God.